TORNADOES!

TORNADOES!

by Sally Rose

SCHOLASTIC INC.
New York Toronto London Auckland Sydney
Mexico City New Delhi Hong Kong

ACKNOWLEDGMENTS
The publisher is grateful to the following individuals for permission to reproduce their photographs and drawings:

Cover and photo insert: NOAA. Interior photos: Bill Bunting, Sue Harrison, David Hoadley, Al Moller, National Weather Service.

Special thanks to the following for permission to use the first-hand accounts found in chapter six: Amanda Lynn Rivera and David Hoadley.

And special thanks to Eileen Kelly-Gallagher and the Cyprus Elementary School, Glenn Field at NWS Taunton, Ted Kaehler, and Al Moller.

ISBN 0-439-27080-4

Published by Scholastic Inc., 555 Broadway, New York, NY 10012, by arrangement with Simon Spotlight, an imprint of Simon & Schuster Children's Publishing Division. "The Weather Channel" is a registered trademark of The Weather Channel, Inc. used under license.

12 11 10 9 8 7 6 5 4 3 2 1 0 1 2 3 4 5/0

Printed in the U.S.A. 23

First Scholastic printing, December 2000

Contents

1

Outbreak!

The people of Manila, Arkansas, could hear the storm coming, but they couldn't see it. It was 3 A.M. on Thursday, April 17, 1998. It sounded like a freight train was bearing down on the town, located 230 miles west of Nashville, Tennessee. The **tornado** was hidden by the early morning darkness and the downpour of rain. When it came, it shattered windows in hundreds of buildings, tore off roofs, and ripped apart mobile homes.

An hour later and 50 miles away, a **twister** left a mobile home park in Roellen, Tennessee in partial ruin. At 6 P.M. that evening another tornado hit Wayne County on the Alabama border.

The following afternoon, two more tornadoes struck Nashville. The first cut a path of destruction through the city almost four miles long. The second struck east of the city. Uprooted trees, downed power lines and pieces from ripped-apart houses and barns were scattered about the streets. "I feel like I've just played the lead in the movie *Twister*," said a salesman who, with his twelve-year-old son, tried to outrun the storm in his pickup truck. "We looked back, and the wind was coming from two different directions. The thing was coming straight down Highway 70."

At Cornelia Fort Airpark in east

Nashville, the fleet of thirty Cessnas and other small airplanes were tossed by the storm and broke apart like cheap plastic toys. "I was looking out the front window of the building, and I saw a Cessna 150 do a back flip toward the building," said the director of the airpark. "I took a dive because I thought it was coming through the plate glass window. It landed right in front of it."

The governor of Tennessee declared Nashville a disaster area. Hundreds of homes were destroyed. The capitol building was among several state buildings that were badly damaged. A bulldozer had to be brought in to help the Metro-Nashville fire department uncover some of its emergency equipment trapped under the wreckage.

The Tennessee Oilers' new football stadium, still in the process of being built, was also damaged. "Parts of the stadium were being tossed around like Popsicle sticks.

I've never seen anything like it," said a man in a nearby restaurant who witnessed the twister as it ravaged the stadium.

Stormy Season

The tornadoes in this outbreak caused a lot of damage in the four states of Arkansas, Illinois, Kentucky, and Tennessee. This outbreak was part of a very active storm season.

El Niño helped make 1998 ripe for severe thunderstorms in the southeastern United States. El Niño is the warming of the water in the central and eastern tropical Pacific Ocean that influences weather patterns all across the globe. By the end of April 1998, six tornado outbreaks had already caused much damage and killed more than one hundred people.

Most tornadoes don't last very long, and don't cause the level of destruction that the

1998 storms did. New technology helps make better and better equipment. This equipment helps forecasters make more accurate **forecasts,** which gives people time to find a safe place to ride out a storm.

Local Storm

A tornado, also called a "twister," produces some of the most powerful winds in nature. But it wields its power in a very localized, or small, area. Most tornadoes are less than fifty yards wide and travel less than a mile. In rare instances, a tornado

Did You Know?

A tornado's effect is usually limited to a local area. A tornado can destroy one side of a street and leave the other alone. There have been reports of leaves and bark being stripped from one side of a tree and left untouched on the other. People have reported being stripped naked by a tornado—but left unhurt.

may reach one mile across and travel many miles. In contrast, hurricanes can be hundreds of miles across and travel for thousands of miles.

The Truth About Twisters: Tornado Facts

- The United States has more tornadoes than any other country in the world.

- Texas, a very large state, has the highest average annual number of tornadoes in the United States. But in Oklahoma a higher concentration of tornadoes occurs per unit area.

- All fifty states have reported tornadoes, but they are rare in the West.

- May and June are the most active months for tornadoes, but they can occur in any month of the year.

- The word tornado comes from the word *tronada*, which means thunderstorm in Spanish.

- Many tornadoes travel at about 30 miles per hour, the speed people typically drive their cars around town. But some can travel up to 60 miles per hour, like a car speeding down the highway.

- Before 1952, forecasters did not use the word tornado in their reports because they were afraid people would panic.

2

The Right Ingredients

Tornadoes often look like huge, spinning funnels. A funnel is a hollow conelike shape, wide at the top and narrow at the bottom. These spinning funnels can form in any thunderstorm, if conditions are right.

Not all thunderstorms produce tornadoes. So what happens to make conditions just right for a tornado to form? Scientists don't yet know all the facts. But here's what they do know:

Building Blocks

Thunderclouds form because warm rising air, called an **updraft**, cools as it travels upward. The moisture, or **water vapor**, condenses into water droplets which appear as clouds. Warm, moist updrafts feed a storm and make the thunderheads grow. The updraft will keep rising as long as it is warmer than its surroundings. Eventually, falling rain or **hail** cools the updrafts feeding the storm. And the thunderclouds begin to fade.

Most thunderstorms last about thirty minutes. As one storm dies out, another storm may start up nearby. Each storm is called a cell. When several thunderstorms form one after another, they are called multicell thunderstorms.

Super Storm

Supercells are intense thunderstorms that can exist for hours. They are the king of all thunderstorms. In **supercell thunderstorms,** the updraft is slightly tilted and rises up above the cold **downdrafts,** so that the cold downdraft can't cut off the updraft of moist air. The storm keeps going as long as there is a fresh supply of warm, moist air. The moving air in a supercell also begins to rotate. This type of powerful storm can produce very strong tornadoes.

The Wind Factor

Winds can blow from different directions and at different speeds at increasing heights in the atmosphere. Changing wind direction and speed are necessary ingredients for tornado formation.

The varying winds in a supercell cause part of it to rotate. The rotating column of air in the supercell is called a **mesocyclone.** Together with updrafts and downdrafts, the mesocyclone helps put the spin in a twister.

Did You Know?

Tornado Alley

There is a place in the central United States where conditions are most favorable for creating tornadoes. This place is called "Tornado Alley," because so many of these violent storms form there.

Tornado Alley extends from Texas up to Nebraska and Iowa. In the spring, this area is the meeting place for three kinds of air—warm, humid air that travels north from the Gulf of Mexico, cold air that comes down from Canada, and dry air that comes east from the Rocky Mountains. This convergence of warm, humid air and cold, dry air makes conditions just right for the formation of severe thunderstorms—and tornadoes!

The Making of a Tornado

Sometimes conditions in a thunderstorm are just right for a tornado to form. All the ingredients are in place. Here's how it might happen:

It's a bright spring day in Tornado Alley. The sun is shining. A warm, humid wind is blowing in from the south at ground level. As the surface of the earth heats up, it further warms the air just above it. Warm, moist air tends to rise up through the atmosphere. But when there is a layer of warm, dry air above it, holding the warm, moist air near the ground, the air below can get warmer and more humid. Eventually the moist air near the ground is able to burst through the layer of warm, dry air.

As the mass of warm, moist air rises, it cools and condenses, forming clouds. This is where the changing wind direction and speed come into play.

Winds from the south interact with the rising air. As the air moves higher, faster winds from the southwest influence it, too. As it rises even higher, dry wind from the west joins in, blowing even faster. All these different winds blowing from different directions and at different speeds provide an environment which supports the development of rotation of the mesocyclone. If some of the spinning air is drawn into a downdraft, it begins to spin faster and faster as it heads toward the ground. The rising updraft then stretches the spiraling column further—eventually forming a tornado!

Did You Know?

Not all supercell thunderstorms produce tornadoes, and not all mesocyclones turn into tornadoes. Scientists are still trying to figure out what makes a particular supercell produce a twister.

It's Just a Stage

Like people, tornadoes typically go through stages in their lives, including the following:

Dust Whirl: Stage 1

Dust and dirt get blown upward in a swirling motion by the rotating column of air which is now in contact with the ground. The air spirals up from the ground to the cloud. A **funnel cloud** sometimes can be seen at this stage, as **condensation** begins to form.

Organizing: Stage 2

In the organizing stage, the funnel, which is now visible, may reach to the ground. It gets bigger and bigger and picks up more and more dust. It may actually look ropelike in this stage. Many tornadoes lose their get-up-and-go at this point and start to shrink. However if the funnel keeps building strength, the tornado will progress to the next stage.

MATURE: STAGE 3

The tornado grows to full size and strength at this stage. It is almost vertical, or straight up and down. The inflow of air at the ground is at its strongest in this stage. Sometimes, more than one funnel can form. Winds can reach over 250 miles per hour. Dirt, houses, cars, big trucks, animals, and anything else in the tornado's path can get caught up in the powerful winds.

SHRINKING: STAGE 4

At this time the tornado's width gets narrower. The tornado may begin to tilt because its bottom moves slower than its top. But although the tornado gets smaller, the winds remain very powerful, possibly even gaining speed. Think of it like a spinning ice-skater who, when pulling in his or her arms, can spin faster and faster.

Decaying: Stage 5

In the decaying stage, the tornado often looks ropelike—stretched and twisted—similar to what saltwater taffy looks like as it's being made. As cool rain falls in the tornado, it cuts off the warm, moist, rising air that was feeding it. Sometimes a second tornado may start up as the first one dies.

Did You Know?

More than one thousand tornadoes form each year on average in the United States.

3

A Twister by Any Other Name

Tornadoes come in many styles, shapes, and sizes. But, in general, tornadoes that form in thunderstorms other than supercells tend to be weaker and short-lived.

Landspouts and Gustnadoes

The most devastating tornadoes are usually produced by supercell thunderstorms.

But any thunderstorm can spawn a tornado if the weather conditions are right. Landspouts are a type of circulation that usually are associated with non-supercell thunderstorms. They are typically weaker than their supercell counterparts.

Landspouts form when winds from different directions come together in the same area where there is a strong updraft. A weak twister is created but it rarely lasts long.

When rain-cooled air in the downdraft hits the ground, it spreads out in all directions. The leading edge of this cool air is called the **gust front.** Circulations called gustnadoes often form in the gust front area, just ahead of a thunderstorm. Gustnadoes don't last long and are usually quite weak. Since the circulating column of air in a gustnado does not typically extend all the way to the clouds above, there is debate as to whether they are truly tornadoes.

Waterspouts

A **waterspout** is a type of tornado that forms over water. They usually form under a fast-growing **cumulus** cloud—puffy, pillowy clouds that can turn into thunderheads. The cumulus cloud may never grow into a thunderstorm, but it can produce a watery little twister. A thin circulation stretches from the water surface (where it kicks up a circle of spray) to the cumulus cloud above. A waterspout almost always poops out when it hits land. But waterspouts can still be dangerous to small boats and yachts.

Did You Know?

Sometimes tornadoes form over land, then travel over water such as a bay or lake. This type of tornado can suck up lots of water, plus anything else that happens to be there. After one of these storms, people have reported seeing it rain fish and frogs!

Other Whirlwinds

Dust devils

On a hot, sunny day in the desert, a light breeze can sometimes kick up a whirling dust devil. A dust devil is a swirling spiral of dust with winds typically not much faster than 25 miles per hour. Usually individual ones don't last long, but they can form repeatedly for hours. A dust devil goes by many names: dancing dervish, desert devil, sand devil, and in Australia they are called "willy-willies."

Snow devils

Snow devils, also called snowspouts, are small, snowy whirls similar to dust devils. They usually occur in high mountain areas but have been spotted in snow-covered country from Antarctica to Greenland.

Steam Devils

Whirling steam devils usually occur over warm bodies of water when the air above is cold, such as over lakes in late fall or in wintertime.

Firewhirls

A firewhirl is a tornado-like spinning column of smoke and fire. The fierce heat caused by a forest fire or a volcanic eruption can create a firewhirl. The winds in a firewhirl can reach 100 miles per hour.

Did You Know?

Stormy Colors

Depending on conditions in the atmosphere and on the ground, sometimes a tornado will take on the color of the dust and soil it's blowing across. In areas where the soil contains red clay, the sky has looked as if it were bleeding during a tornado.

4

The Strongest Winds on Earth

As a tornado whirls and whirls, it stirs up powerful winds. Some of the fastest wind speeds on earth are found in the most powerful tornadoes. Tornado winds have been estimated at over 250 miles per hour. But it is rare for a tornado to reach that strength.

Most tornadoes don't last very long and are relatively weak. About 75 percent of the tornadoes that touch down in the

Did You Know?

A hurricane's winds rarely reach over 155 miles per hour. Most of the deaths caused by hurricanes are from storm surges as well as flooding caused by heavy rainfall. A storm surge occurs when the wind piles up water from the ocean, lakes, or bays and pushes it onto land.

United States last less than 15 minutes. They are only 50 yards across, and they travel only a mile or two. Once in a while, though, huge monster-size tornadoes are born that can last for several hours, measure up to a mile or more across, and travel more than 100 miles. Tornadoes like these can cause lots of damage if they strike a town or city.

Did You Know?

In terms of energy per unit of space, a tornado is the strongest storm in nature.

Mr. Tornado

For a long time, there was no way to measure the strength of a tornado. But then Dr. Theodore Fujita, a scientist originally from Japan, invented a scale that rates the intensity of a tornado by the amount of damage it causes to man-made structures. The scale is now called the Fujita Scale of Tornado Intensity.

Fujita Scale of Tornado Intensity

Rating	Wind Speed (miles per hour)	Damage
F-0	40 to 72 mph	light
F-1	73 to 112 mph	moderate
F-2	113 to 157 mph	considerable
F-3	158 to 206 mph	severe
F-4	207 to 260 mph	devastating
F-5	261 to 318 mph	incredible

The Fujita Scale contains six levels, from F-0 to F-5. Very few tornadoes reach F-5 strength. Of the 25,000 tornadoes recorded in the U.S. between 1916 and 1979, Dr. Fujita rated only 127 of them at F-5.

Did You Know?

Dr. Fujita came up with his damage scale in the late 1960s after taking many plane rides to investigate storm damage. He was nicknamed "Mr. Tornado" in a 1972 *National Geographic* article. Ten years after the article was published Dr. Fujita finally witnessed his first tornado firsthand.

OUTSTANDING TORNADOES THROUGHOUT HISTORY

Tornadoes often occur in groups, called "outbreaks." Here are some of the most famous outbreaks in history:

The Great Natchez Tornado, May 7, 1840—A violent tornado hit Natchez, Mississippi, a little port on the Mississippi

River. Although the worst of the considerable damage was over within five minutes, the tornado kept churning through the city for almost half an hour. Of the 317 people killed, 269 were on boats on the Mississippi River. Some reports say the width of the tornado completely encompassed the mile-wide city, and then some.

The Great Southern Outbreak, February 19, 1884—More than sixty tornadoes ravaged the Southeast, from Mississippi to Virginia between 10 A.M. and midnight. At least 170 people were killed, possibly more. It was considered the largest outbreak until the Super Outbreak in April 1974.

The Tri-State Tornado, March 18, 1925—This was the deadliest tornado episode in U.S. history: a total of 747 people died. Most of the damage was done by one tornado, which traveled for three and a

(Sue Harrison)

This red truck, among other things, was destroyed by a tornado that hit Chiefland, Florida, in March 1993.

(Al Moller)

Huge tornado outside Red Rock, Oklahoma, on April 26, 1991. Although this tornado was officially rated an F4, it created the highest winds ever recorded on earth, 287 mph, which were measured by a portable Doppler radar.

(David Hoadley)

(David Hoadley)

This series of images shows a tornado forming west of Hodges, Texas, on May 13, 1989. At top, the funnel cloud is just connecting with the dust cloud on the ground. At far right, the ground contact portion has moved slowly southwest as the cloud base drifts slowly east northeast, resulting in a stretched vortex.

(David Hoadley)

TORNADO ALLEY

HOT ZONE
Kansas City
Andover
Enid
Norman
Amarillo
Tucson
Wichita Falls
Saragosa
THE WEATHER CHANNEL

(The Weather Channel)

Tornado Alley

This just-formed tornado is approaching a local airport four miles northwest of Pratt, Kansas, on May 25, 1965.

(David Hoadley)

(NWS)

Tornado near Itasca, Texas, in 1976.

(Sue Harrison)

Damage to brick home by March 1993 tornado in Chiefland, Florida.

A wet microburst forming just east of Pauls Valley, Oklahoma. Wet microbursts are often mistaken for tornadoes.

(NWS)

(Bill Bunting)

Tornadoes often form from this type of anvil-shaped wall cloud.

(NOAA)

This tornado struck Union City, Oklahoma, on May 24, 1973.

(NOAA)

Tornado near Seymour, Texas, in April 1979.

half hours over 219 miles across Missouri, Illinois, and Indiana, and killed 695 people.

The Tupelo-Gainesville Outbreak, April 5-6, 1936—This was the second deadliest outbreak ever recorded. Seventeen tornadoes killed 446 people, most of them in Tupelo, Mississippi, and Gainesville, Georgia, and injured more than 2,300. The first one hit in the evening on April 5, and they continued to wreak destruction through the following morning.

The Wichita Falls Tornado, April 10, 1979—This was one of the most destructive tornadoes in U.S. history. Forty-five people were killed and 1,740 injured. More than 3,000 homes were destroyed and 20,000 people were left homeless.

The Pennsylvania-Ohio Outbreak, May 31, 1985—Forty-one tornadoes that hit

Ohio, Pennsylvania, New York, and Ontario, Canada, made this the worst recorded tornado outbreak in the region. Seventy-six people were killed in the U.S., and the damage totaled over $450 million.

Central Florida outbreak, February 22-23, 1998—Tornadoes tipping the Fujita Scale at F-3 tore through central Florida between midnight and 1 A.M. killing forty-two people and leaving hundreds homeless. It was the worst outbreak in the area's history. Fourteen counties were declared federal disaster areas.

The Super Outbreak

On April 3, 1974, a mass of cold air was bringing snow to the Rocky Mountains. In the Gulf of Mexico the water was 75 degrees Fahrenheit. Water was evaporating into the warm air making the air above the

Gulf humid and moist. The ingredients were all in place for the creation of some violent tornadoes.

Intense thunderstorms developed quickly the afternoon of April 3. These thunderstorms gave birth to an astonishing 148 tornadoes that struck in 14 states, the majority occurring from Indiana and Ohio to Alabama. The outbreak finally ended in West Virginia and Virginia, early in the morning of the 4th. This event came to be called the Super Outbreak. It is still the largest number of tornadoes on record produced by one storm system. More than 300 people lost their lives; more than 6,000 people were injured. Thirty of the twisters were rated at F-4 or F-5, and 48 of them were killer storms.

Did You Know?

Tornadoes cause an average of $1 billion worth of property damage in the United States each year.

5

Forecasting and Storm Tracking

Tornadoes are the hardest kind of severe weather to forecast. Weather scientists try to predict when a severe storm will hit so people in the area can reach safety in time. In tornado country, most people have storm cellars where they can take refuge during a storm.

Even with today's advanced technology, weather forecasters can tell only about twenty minutes ahead of when a tornado might hit.

Tools of the Trade

Scientists use all sorts of tools to predict when a bad storm will hit. One of the instruments they use is called "radar." Radar stands for radio detection and ranging. One type of radar scientists use is called **Doppler radar.** It tells scientists which way and how fast air is moving. Doppler radar can "see" inside a cloud.

Scientists also use portable Doppler radar to measure the wind speeds in a tornado. With a portable Doppler, researchers can put the radar near the path of the storm and then retreat to safety.

Satellite photographs taken from space also help to predict approaching weather. Satellites take pictures of the clouds above Earth at regular intervals, usually every half hour. They can help tell exactly where thunderstorms are occurring. Some satellites can measure the temperature at the top of the clouds, the height of waves in the ocean, the temperature of the sea surface, and the speed of the wind.

Computers at the National Weather Service (NWS) help researchers put all of the information together so that forecasters can make predictions and send out storm watches or warnings.

Did You Know?

In a study called VORTEX, scientists gathered lots of information by driving and flying near supercell storms. Weather scientists are still using this information to figure out why some supercell thunderstorms produce tornadoes and some don't.

Storm Chasers

Most people seek safety when a tornado

hits. But some adventurous folks chase after storms in their cars or vans. Some chasers are scientists who collect information for organizations like the National Severe Storms Laboratory in Norman, Oklahoma. Some chasers are photographers or videographers who take pictures to sell to television news shows or magazines or books. And some chasers are thrill seekers who enjoy seeing a tornado grow out of a cloud and being in danger's way.

Did You Know?

There's an old weather saying, "A pale green sky means the wind is high," which is one way to say the sky turns green just before a tornado forms. Some still believe this is a good predictor.

STORM SPOTTER NETWORKS

Weather forecasters use a network of **storm spotters** to help them predict where a tornado might hit. Storm spotters are regular people with ham (short-wave) radios who volunteer to keep an eye out for possible storms in their area.

Scientists rely on spotters to tell them what's going on in a storm between the ground and the base of the cloud. Forecasters at NWS can't see this area with their Doppler radar. Spotters turn in reports via their ham radios to local network managers, who then report back to scientists at the NWS.

Spotters provide important information about the size of hail, the direction the wind is blowing, and whether **downbursts** are occurring. The NWS uses that information to send out updates on a storm's location and which way it is headed. A watch or warning might also be issued.

Weather forecasters will issue a tornado watch for an area in which conditions are ripe for tornadoes to form. If forecasters issue a tornado warning, it means that tornadoes have actually been seen in the area or indicated on radar.

Forrest Mitchell, a ham radio operator and a scientist with the NWS in Norman, Oklahoma, says that many spotter groups also have other duties, including rescue and relief efforts after a storm has hit. And their ham radios are often used as backup communication because phone lines may be down, and even cell phone service may be interrupted.

Did You Know?

According to tradition, Apache Indians used to fill transparent animal skins with bear grease in order to predict the weather. The cloudlike patterns that formed in the grease were read as signs. One Apache man from Cloudcraft, New Mexico, says he saw "tornado patterns" in his bear grease the day before eight tornadoes hit an area in the midwestern United States.

WEB SITE ADDRESSES

There are many places on the Internet where information about tornadoes can be found. The Weather Channel's home page is an excellent source of up-to-the-minute forecasts and late-breaking news about tornadoes and other types of severe weather, with colorful photos and maps. You can find it at:

http://www.weather.com

Here are some other Web sites that contain lots of fascinating facts and neat graphics.

http://www.tornadoproject.com
The Tornado Project is a company that compiles all types of information on tornadoes and includes resources for videos and books on tornadoes. This site contains moderate graphics and great links to other tornado sites.

http://tesla.theforge.com/tornado

This is another page from the Tornado Project Online that offers information on recent tornadoes, tornadoes in history, myths, safety, stories, questions and answers, videos, books and posters, and lots of graphics.

http://taiga.geog.niu.edu/chaser/tortalk.html

Tornado Talk is a Web page put together by storm chasers that includes articles on storm chasing ethics, chasing safety tips, videography, and photography tips.

http://www.geocities.com/CapeCanaveral/Lab/2430/tornado.html

This site offers information on tornado formation, the Fujita Scale, and safety, plus photos of tornadoes and tornado damage.

http://redrock.ncsa.uiuc.edu/PATHFINDER/aisrp93/storm_research/tornado.html

This is a university site with information on tornado research, including supercell and nonsupercell tornado computer simulation, with colorful graphics of simulations.

http://www.nssl.noaa.gov/

This is the homepage for the National Severe Storms Laboratory with links to current research and other neat sites, plus answers to commonly asked questions and information on careers in weather.

6

Personal Stories

On February 23, 1998, seven tornadoes hit central Florida. Forty-two people were killed, hundreds of people were injured. Winds estimated to be between 158 to 206 miles per hour tore away walls and roofs, threw cars on tops of houses, and leveled a strip mall. Houses in many neighborhoods were left in rubble. Others were untouched. It was considered the deadliest outbreak in Florida's history.

The counties of Orange, Osceola, Seminole, and Volusia were hardest hit. Children from Cypress Elementary School in Kissimmee, in Osceola County, wrote of their experiences during the storms as a class project. Their accounts were written two months after the tornado struck. One of their stories is included here.

Amanda's Story

"On Monday I was sleeping. And then . . . my mom woke up and heard a noise. It sounded like a train. She woke Dad, my brother, and me. My mom seemed to be scared. I was scared, too, because I didn't know what was happening. When my mom woke me up, I heard a lot of heavy rain and it was really windy.

While I was in the bathroom, I heard a lot of things. I heard the blinds in all of the rooms hitting the walls, the sofas in the living room were being thrown against the walls. I heard glass breaking, the pots and pans in the kitchen were banging around. I heard our garage door break and the alarms for the cars were all going off. I heard doors being slammed closed. My dog, Gambit, was barking a lot. Me and my brother and my mom and dad were all in the bathroom together.

After it was done, my mom and dad looked around the house. They saw glass everywhere and glass on the beds. The house was all destroyed except my brother's room. His bed was fine. His toys were in place.

My mom told me that the walls in my room were cracked and all the windows were broken. A part of our roof was missing. Some of my clothes and shoes were gone. Some of my toys were wet from the rain and some of them flew away. My bed was tilted and facing the window and had glass all over it.

When the tornado was coming my dog was barking at the windows. . . . My dad picked him up and put him in the bathroom with us. My mom put my rabbit in a box with some food and water. My rabbit survived. His name is Charlie. My mom got glass stuck in her foot, but she is okay.

We stayed at my mom's friend's house until our house was fixed up and safe again."

— Amanda, age 8

David Hoadley is a storm chaser who lives in Virginia. This is an experience he had while chasing tornadoes in 1993 with his nineteen-year-old daughter, Sarah.

David's Story

"On June 6, we were in northeast

Colorado and heard a report on the car radio of a tornado forecast for southern Nebraska. It was early evening before we reached that area and began hearing reports of tornadoes on the ground west of Kearney. However, a rain shield blocked our view and the setting sun didn't help visibility. Frustrated at missing those storms, I reached Interstate 80 just as a new radio bulletin warned of a tornado approaching the small town of Amherst. We found a county road to Amherst. Now [it was] completely dark. We drove through a gusting west wind and moderate rain. We hadn't seen any dangerous clouds, and I assumed the Amherst tornado was long gone.

Big mistake!

Since I didn't want to drive into a damaged town at night and risk a flat tire from nails in broken boards, we turned around. Just as I was accelerating, the wind began to swing cyclonically around from the west, from the south, and then from the east. Ground fog instantly formed all around us like a legion of ghosts, but it was quickly swept up in the rapidly increasing wind. I stopped, and the headlights now showed horizontal sheets of wind-whipped rain. Next, I heard a steadily increasing "whoosh" sound to the west and instantly knew a tornado was moving right at us.

Such a storm can quickly turn a car into a crushed and twisted clump of metal. I said to Sarah, 'In the ditch, now!' We struggled to open the doors against the wind. I ran around the car, jumped in the ditch in the wet grass beside her, and watched the car to be sure it didn't blow in our direction.

Fortunately, the tornado was just forming and the car was not moved or damaged. Other than my daughter receiving some minor leg scratches, we were uninjured.

Thoroughly soaked, we again began driving. The west wind increased with even heavier rain, and soon nothing could be seen in front of the car. My daughter was terrified. I knew the worst of the danger had passed. Strong west winds are normal behind a tornado, which meant it was moving away.

There are several reasons why I misjudged the storm. One was that I failed to switch from AM to FM radio for current weather bulletins. The AM reception was blanked out by lightning static; an FM station might have reported that the storm was still strong (despite rainy west wind, which usually means it's weakening) and had become a 'right turner,' headed directly for us. Experience is sometimes the best teacher, if we survive it!"

— David Hoadley, storm chaser, Falls Church, Virginia

Web site address

http://tqjunior.advanced.org/4232/

Thinkquest Junior is a site for tornado enthusiasts, it has information on tornadoes, survivor stories, and a place for other tornado survivors to share their experiences, plus a photo gallery. This site also contains colorful and animated graphics.

7

Tornado Safety

Safety during a tornado is very important. If you live in an area frequented by tornadoes, your home and school should have tornado safety plans in place. Schools in areas that experience a lot of tornadoes usually conduct regular drills.

Here are some things to do to stay safe when a tornado is threatening nearby:

1. Stay tuned to television or radio broadcasts about tornado watches and warnings in your area. Be prepared to take cover. Stay away from windows. The basement is the safest place to be during a tornado. Make sure you are not under a place where there is a heavy piece of furniture, such as a refrigerator, on the floor above you. If you don't have a basement, seek shelter in a closet or in a bathroom in the middle of your house.

2. Protect your head and eyes from flying objects and pieces of broken glass by wrapping yourself in a blanket.

3. Keep disaster supplies, such as flashlights, a transistor radio, candles, matches, medicines, extra batteries, nonperishable food, basic tools, and

baby necessities in a spot that everybody knows about. If you think your water supply might be interrupted, store drinking water in clean, covered containers or in bathtubs.

4 If you are at school during a tornado, stay away from rooms with wide roofs that might collapse, such as gymnasiums and auditoriums. Take shelter near an inside wall on the lowest floor, kneel on the floor facing the wall and protect your head with your hands and arms.

5 If you live in a mobile home, leave immediately and go to a public shelter or to a neighbor's basement. Mobile homes are not anchored well to a foundation and can be damaged or lifted by tornadoes. Seek shelter in a solid, structured building or, if necessary,

in a ditch. You are less likely to be touched by a tornado if you are lying flat in a ditch than if you stay in a mobile home.

6 Do not stay in your car if you see a tornado approaching. Get out immediately and seek shelter in a building or in a ditch. Never try to outrun a tornado in your car.

7 If you are in an open field, quickly take cover in a low-lying area such as a ditch. Lay face down, covering your head if possible, for protection from flying objects.

Remember: Lightning often occurs during a tornadic thunderstorm. Avoid touching metal objects, such as a wire fence, and stay away from tall trees and open water. Do not use the telephone, take a shower or a bath during a tornado or a lightning storm.

Web site addresses

There are many places on the Internet where information about tornado safety can be found. Here are some Web sites that contain lots of important facts and helpful tips on what to do before, during, and after a tornado hits your area:

http://www.weather.com/safeside/
or
http://www.redcross.org/safeside/

The Weather Channel and Red Cross have teamed up to create the national safety and preparedness initiative called Project Safeside: Keeping You Ahead of the Storm. These two sites, one sponsored by The Weather Channel and the other by the Red Cross, have important safety tips for how to prepare for a storm and what to do when it hits. Both have colorful graphics and photos.

http://www.redcross.org/disaster/safety/tornados.html

Red Cross site shows how to prepare a home tornado plan and assemble a disaster supply kit, and debunks some common myths about tornadoes. Colorful graphics.

http://www.nws.noaa.gov/om/tornado.htm

National Weather Service site offers information about tornadoes and safety tips, with links to full-color graphics.

http://www.dem.dcc.state.nc.us/pio/tor.htm#2

North Carolina state site has information on tornadoes and their destructive forces and safety tips, not many graphics.

http://www.fema.gov/library/tornadof.htm

Fact sheet from Federal Emergency Management Agency (FEMA) with virtual library and electronic reading room, with safety tips. Some graphics.

GLOSSARY

CONDENSATION—Water in the form of gas, called water vapor, cools and turns into the liquid form of water, or water droplets.

CUMULUS—Fluffy, cottony clouds that are usually seen in good weather.

DOPPLER RADAR—An instrument that can measure the speed and direction of moving air.

DOWNBURST—Wind that blasts down from a thunderstorm.

DOWNDRAFT—A strong current of air that heads from within a storm cloud toward the ground.

FORECAST—To predict, or tell ahead of time.

FUNNEL CLOUD—A rotating funnellike column of air and associated cloud extending down from a cloud but not reaching the ground.

GUST FRONT—Wind near the ground moving away from a thunderstorm, usually on the leading edge of the storm.

HAIL—Frozen chunks of ice that form in updrafts, or rising currents of air, during thunderstorms.

MESOCYCLONE—Rotating air associated with a supercell thunderstorm, from which tornadoes can form.

ROTATE—To move around in a circular motion.

STORM CHASERS—People who try to get as close as possible to severe weather systems, such as thunderstorms, tornadoes, and hurricanes, in order to study or photograph them.

STORM SPOTTERS—Volunteers all over the country that keep an eye on the weather conditions, and pass on information to the National Weather Service about severe storms and tornadoes in their area.

SUPERCELL THUNDERSTORM—A powerful thunderstorm with rotating air motions that can give rise to strong tornadoes.

TORNADO—A violently rotating column of air that extends from a storm cloud to the ground.

TWISTER—Another name for a tornado.

UPDRAFT—A strong current of air that moves upward through a storm cloud.

WATERSPOUT—A weak tornado that forms over a body of water, from a fast-growing cumulus cloud to the water below.

WATER VAPOR—Water in the form of an invisible gas.

WHIRLWIND—A general term for a rotating column of air. Examples include tornadoes and dust devils.

Index